MW01484084

Two Tyrants

*The Myth of a Two-Party Government and the
Liberation of the American Voter*

A.G. Roderick

- City of Gold Publishing -

Published by
City of Gold Publishing
First printing: 2015

ISBN: 978-0990889205

For my amazing wife.
Thanks for being my eternal partner in crime
and
my intellectual muse.

Contents

About the Author

A.G. Roderick is a freelance writer and former staff writer for a top 10 American newspaper. He has worked as a legislative analyst and policy advisor in multiple state legislatures and at the municipal level. He holds a Bachelors Degree in International Relations and a Masters Degree in Public Policy from Michigan State University.

Introduction

Modern American elections have turned citizens into subjects, and the two major parties into de facto dictators. The Republicans and Democrats have won every presidential election since 1853. Fidel Castro must have taken inspiration from such electoral dominance in plotting his own presidential designs.

Our current election process suffocates those of independent thought. It whispers that we have but two unfortunate options from which to choose. Any system in which the likes of Al Sharpton and Sarah Palin hold any political influence is glaringly obsolete and begs to be replaced.

Ironically, our system is one of the most un-American electoral schemes on Earth. It favors the powerful over the weak. It promotes oligarchy. It allows two morally bankrupt syndicates to dictate our political destiny. Operating in a state of symphonic polarization, Democrats and Republicans have achieved absolute power.

The goal of this book is not to decry the evils of political parties. Participation or lack thereof in any political party should be a decision left up to the individual. The Republican and Democratic parties have an opportunity serve a useful purpose in our society. However they can only do so if their power is checked by a system that promotes political access. The current structure is ruled by political exclusivity, bolstered by the two parties and their surrogates.

Powerful ideas should require minimal explanation. As such, this work is intended to serve as a model for impact in brevity. It falls somewhere between a political missive and a non-fiction novella. *More* words written of our political ills are not needed. *New* words expressing alternative ideas will be the cure to what ails us. Therefore, delving into the endless mundanities of public policy is not attempted herein.

Broad problems with policymaking are addressed and explained, but the minutia is left for others. The goal of maintaining a big picture focus is to make the content accessible to all. The two major parties have benefited for too long from a populace that accepts the inevitability of its own ignorance. That's why redistribution of information is more vital now than redistribution of wealth or any other resource. This book is written for the average American, and is structured to that end.

Two Tyrants is a call to arms for Americans tired of suffering in the political Matrix. It is fair warning to all who support the current electoral shell game. It is a clarion call to voters of every persuasion: You have a role to play in restoring the promise of our democracy; take your places.

Chapter I

Pick Your Poison

I

State of the Union

Two thieving corporations have hijacked our government — modern day exemplars of corruption and ego that could have provoked the envy of Julius Caesar himself. For over a century, the Democratic and Republican parties have won virtually every election in America. They hold the presidency of the United States. They maintain control of the US House of Representatives, the US Senate, 49 of 50 state legislatures and all 50 state governorships. They reign over all — their power a result of a preferential voting process and a uniquely American political psychosis.

An unflinching belief in the power of the individual has always been one of our republic's greatest virtues. We no longer adhere to this principle in modern political life. We promote and adulate two power-hungry collectives based on a false premise of common values. These two parties do not represent America's independent political legacy. They represent lies and pervasive societal lethargy. They represent a broken system that stifles the innovative and rewards the banal. They represent tyranny.

An oft-quoted colonial witticism asks if it is better to be ruled by one tyrant three thousand miles away, or three thousand tyrants one mile away. The statement is a commentary on the ironic similarities of self-rule and colonialism. While an astute observation for its time, the question makes no mention of our current predicament. We are now ruled by *two tyrants*, and they are everywhere. They operate under an implied power-sharing agreement, keeping any outside competition at bay. They are our masters, and we their patrons. We are three hundred million drifting souls — hungry ghosts seemingly damned to a life of political impotence.

Laws of Diminishing Returns

A review of Republican and Democratic policy achievements over the last 25 years is a master class in buffoonery. Control of Congress and the presidency has consistently changed hands in the last two and a half decades. Unfortunately, for all the biennial bluster of new beginnings, change never comes.

In the last 100 years, neither party has gone more

than 12 years without a term in the presidency. We've become accustomed to the rotting stench of their incompetence. That only two parties truly participate in our politics is a disgrace. Three common domestic policy concerns highlight the dire straits in which we now find ourselves.

Educational accomplishment, social mobility, and economic stability should be bastions of American accomplishment. The first two of these issues refer exclusively to individual opportunity and freedom. Successes in the first two areas often lead to success in the 3rd. In other words, an educated populace can readily enjoy the benefit of upward mobility. Such a relationship typically yields a robust and dynamic economy. Such has not been the case in recent history.

Educational Accomplishment: A 2012 report on 15-year-olds from 65 nations yielded the following sobering results: American students scored below the average in Math. They were not quite average in Science and Reading. US students ranked 30th, 23rd and 20th in Math, Science and Reading, respectively. What's worse, the United States spends more money per student than any other country in the developed world.[i] Our children are ill prepared for the global competition they will increasingly face.

These shameful statistics have some of their roots in the absolutism of our two-party politics. The linchpin of the education policy debate in America is the role of teachers unions. Teachers unions are a wildly wealthy and powerful lobby in America. The majority of their political contributions go to Democratic candidates. As such, Democratic minds become clouded by union cash. The Democratic Party structure is built on the foundation of monetary support by unions. Therefore, for Democrats to maintain the influx of union money, the good of the unions must be paramount to the good of the students.

Conversely, the Republican Party must take every opportunity to reduce union influence as a means of political resistance against the Democrats. From the Republican perspective, the unions and the Democratic Party are one and the same. Therefore, weakening of the unions is a means of self-preservation. And so it goes for the Republicans, that denying union power must be paramount to the good of the students.

The role and influence of teachers unions is a relevant topic in any education debate. Unfortunately, both parties treat them as the *only* important stakeholder in the conversation. The only real debate happening is whether to come after the teachers unions with torches and pitchforks, or to give them the keys to the kingdom.

Social Mobility: A poor child born in the US today is more likely to become a poor adult than they would have 30 years ago. That likelihood is now higher in the United States than it is in the United Kingdom, which has a millenniums-old aristocratic tradition.[ii] This has more to do with the marriage of the two parties with large corporations than with a changing labor market.

They have both surrendered our right of self-determination to their corporate sponsors. Lack of consistent oversight has allowed corporate profit whoring to diminish the earning potential of the average American worker. Reduced salaries, transference of corporate tax liability, and reductions in employee benefits continue to drain the bank accounts of the average American.

Both parties deal with corporate corruption in vastly different ways. Republicans sing the praises of corporations, and then turn a blind eye to corporate corruption in exchange for campaign donations. Democrats, on the other hand, publicly complain of the unfair influence and inherent evil of corporations. Only *then* do they turn a blind eye to corporate corruption in exchange for campaign donations. Party acceptance of corporate malfeasance has been devastating to Americans' ability to get ahead.

In his 19th century masterwork Democracy in America, Alexis De Tocqueville noted

> Among aristocratic nations, as families remain for centuries in the same condition, often on the same spot, all generations become, as it were, contemporaneous . . . Among democratic nations [like the United States], new families are constantly springing up,

> others are constantly falling away, and all that
> remain   change   their   condition.[iii]

De Tocqueville saw the ease with which Americans traversed social strata as one of the most exceptional traits of our new republic. If we cannot retain our historically fluid sense of social mobility, we will have lost an integral part of our American economic heritage.

Economic Stability: In 2008, the US economy inadvertently broke the world. We have yet to fully recover. The 2008 economic recession was largely a result of both parties' ignorance of (or disinterest in) simple economics. They were more concerned with the next election than with minding the economic shop.

Leading up to the 2008 housing crisis, the Republicans ignored unscrupulous lending practices in the mortgage sector. At the same time, the Democrats championed underprivileged acquisition of real estate, regardless of ability to pay. All the while, both parties reaped untold campaign and personal riches from the housing bubble and their associations with gargantuan lending institutions.

The Great Recession was a finite event that will eventually be charted as a bell curve with a discernible beginning and end. The same cannot be said for our national debt. As of August 2014, The United States national debt was approximately $17 trillion and climbing.[iv] Every president and congressional cohort has been content to ignore the gathering storm. A hotter potato we've not seen. At some point our government and our people will have to pay the piper (and his Chinese counterpart). Regardless of who holds the majority of our debt, it is a burden that only worsens with time.

A debt of such profundity is dangerous and irresponsible. Over time this kind of financial burden leads to a higher cost of living for all Americans. Both parties are responsible for the size of the debt, but neither will suffer the consequences in electoral terms. Our two-party con-job breeds voter apathy on such issues, since neither of our two "choices" is willing to face the problem.

Exporting Failure

The unfettered idiocy of the Democratic and Republican parties is of import to people all over the world. The policies of the US government impact other nations more than those of any other country. Many times this influence is a force for good. Unfortunately, US policy is becoming exceedingly burdensome for a growing number of people around the globe.

A review of the international effects of the afore-mentioned recession highlights this fact. Between 2008 and 2009 the global economy actually contracted. This event, no matter how brief it was, had an immeasurable impact on the livelihoods of millions of people worldwide. The job losses alone constitute a global human tragedy.

The Republican and Democratic parties are completely negligent for this surplus of human suffering, yet neither has been held to account. Both sides continue to sip champagne and eat caviar while the rest of the world is scavenging for scraps.

In addition to the economic impacts of our leadership vacuum, bumbling US defense policy has harmed our status and position worldwide. This is not an indictment of the US military, or the brave souls that risk their lives and sanity in the defense of their American brethren. Those at fault for wrongheaded defense policies are the tyrants, who are more beholden to their moribund ideological mores than they are to reason. Partisan dogma discourages clear thinking on both sides of the aisle in terms of defense policy. This leads to a cavalier treatment of military resources and American souls.

Showing Their Stripes

The two parties currently in charge have no motivation to act with moral or ethical haste. The situation continues to worsen because there is no accountability for their persistent numb-scullery. The current system encourages action without consequences. In the land of the two tyrants, no political sin is too grave for redemption. Punishment is reserved for the individual politician alone. There are no long-term repercussions for the organization that allowed said scoundrel to rise to the highest echelons of American power.

The list of criminal convictions for members of the US House of Representatives and US Senate covering the last four presidents illustrates just how perilous our situation has become (See following pages.).

CRIMINAL CONVICTIONS FOR CONGRESS MEMBERS '89-Present

★ *Republicans* ★

PRESIDENT BARACK OBAMA

'13 **SEN. MIKE CRAPO**
Drunk driving

'13 **SEN. REY RADEL**
Cocaine possession

'13 **REP. RICK RENZI**
17 counts of wire fraud, conspiracy, extortion, racketeering, money laundering and making false statements to insurance regulators

'09 **REP. VITO FOSSELLA**
Drunk driving

PRESIDENT GEORGE W. BUSH

'07 **SEN. LARRY CRAIG**
Arrested for homosexual lewd conduct, resulting in a conviction for disorderly conduct

'07 **REP. BOB NEY**
Conspiracy and making false statements regarding political bribes

'05 **REP. DUKE CUNNINGHAM**
Conspiracy to commit bribery, mail fraud, wire fraud and tax evasion

'03 **REP. BILL JANKLOW**
2nd degree manslaughter

PRESIDENT BILL CLINTON

'97 **REP. WES COOLEY**
Making false statements in campaign materials

'95 **SEN. DAVID DURENBERGER**
Misuse of public funds

PRESIDENT GEORGE H.W. BUSH

'92 **REP. JAY KIM**
Accepting $250,000 in illegal campaign contributions

'92 **REP. BUZ LUKENS**
Bribery, conspiracy and paying a minor for sex

CRIMINAL CONVICTIONS FOR CONGRESS MEMBERS

 '89–Present

★ *Democrats* ★

PRESIDENT
BARACK OBAMA

13 **REP. JESSE JACKSON, JR.**
Wire and mail fraud in connection with his misuse of $750,000 of campaign funds

'09 **REP. WILLIAM J. JEFFERSON**
11 counts of bribery

PRESIDENT
GEORGE W. BUSH

05 **REP. FRANK BALLANCE**
Federal money laundering and mail fraud

'02 **REP. JIM TRAFICANT**
10 felony counts of financial corruption

PRESIDENT
BILL CLINTON

'99 **REP. AUSTIN MURPHY**
Voter fraud for filling out absentee ballots for members of a nursing home

'97 **REP. MEL REYNOLDS**
Sexual assault, obstruction of justice, solicitation of child pornography

'95 **REP. WALTER R. TUCKER III**
Extortion and tax evasion

'95 **REP. JOE KOLTER**
Conspiracy

'95 **REP. DAN ROSTENKOWSKI**
Embezzlement of House Post Office money

'93 **REP. NICHOLAS MAVROULES**
15 counts of extortion and accepting illegal gifts

PRESIDENT
GEORGE H.W. BUSH

'92 **REP. CARL C. PERKINS**
Check kiting scheme involving several financial institutions

'92 **REP. CARROLL HUBBARD**
Illegally funneling money to his wife's 1992 campaign to succeed him in Congress

'92 **REP. MARY ROSE OAKAR**
Misdemeanor campaign finance charge

'92 **REP. ALBERT BUSTAMANTE**
Accepting bribes

'92 **REP. WALTER FAUNTROY**
Filing false disclosure forms in order to hide unauthorized income

A majority of these legislators went to prison for their crimes. The political parties that vouched for them bore no tangible consequences. Of the above 27 Democratic and Republican legislators who resigned in disgrace, two out of three (18 of them) were immediately replaced by another legislator of the same party.[v] This is not so surprising for the three senators on the list because senators are immediately replaced by gubernatorial appointment.

For the 24 convicted House members however, the rules are different. Any time a member of the House of Representatives leaves his or her seat mid-term, a special election must be held in the district to replace them. This means that more often than not the voters of a congressional district will choose to replace a convicted congress-felon with another member of the same party. A closer look at two of these specific situations demonstrates the depths of our sick relationship with the two parties.

As referenced above, in the late 1990's Democratic Congress member Mel Reynolds was removed from his seat and imprisoned for crimes including sexual assault, solicitation of child pornography and obstruction of justice. As his replacement, the voters immediately elected another Democrat, Jesse Jackson Jr. In 2013, Congressman Jackson was also removed from the same seat for misuse of $750,000 of campaign funds; He was convicted and sent to prison. The voters of the district immediately elected *yet another* Democrat to replace

Two Tyrants

Jackson. Regardless of his replacement's qualifications or competence, the lack of party accountability for promoting unethical candidates is cause for grave concern. There exists no deterrent for party involvement with ethically questionable candidates.

Unfortunately the other side of the aisle is no better. In 1992 Republican Representative Buz Lukens was arrested and removed from office for bribery, conspiracy and paying a 16-year-old girl for sex. As it were, the voters replaced him in a special election with (here's a shocker) another Republican. That Republican was John Boehner, future Speaker of the House of Representatives.

To review this pathetic state of affairs, the Democratic Party supported two criminals in a row to represent the people of Chicago. Their punishment was apparently infinite control of that particular congressional seat. Similarly, for *their* support of a criminal congressman, the Republican Party was given another undeserved chance by Ohio voters. That second chance paid off for the party in the form of control of the House speakership. It's no wonder the parties don't respect the authority of voters. Perhaps the "I Voted" stickers handed out at polling stations should be replaced with ones reading "Thank You Sir. May I Have Another?"

A.G. Roderick

Cut From The Same Cloth

The Democrats and Republicans are two sides of the same coin. Their homogeneous ruling strategies have lulled us into a false sense of two-party legitimacy. Americans trust in the authority and legitimacy of the presidency, which gives our society stability. Unfortunately, our perversely transitive brains have transferred that legitimacy from the office itself, to the party of the office-holder.

We hold a presidential election every four years wherein the voters choose primarily between a Republican and a Democrat. We are so accustomed to this arrangement that few question its effectiveness. Other candidates are on the ballot at times, but they are often subject to an unofficial press blackout and are excluded from televised debates. Furthermore, the two options forced upon us every four years are more similar than most recognize. Much of their public debate is merely sound and fury.

Five of the last seven US presidents have attended either Harvard or Yale, going back over 40 years (George W. Bush actually attended both.). The Ivy League has become our very own presidential puppy-mill. Temperament be damned; if the papers verify the pedigree we overlook any obvious intellectual or emotional shortcomings.

This strongly implies that most of our presidents do not live in the real world. They do not deal with typical

American problems. They can only make decisions based on their own aristocratic version of reality, where power is inherited and consequences are minimal. Even those Ivy attendees who come from humbler beginnings often acculturate to their highbrow surroundings.

Intellectual elitist assimilation becomes a means of making connections and getting ahead in such an environment. We have not elected a non Ivy League president for over a quarter of a century. This is an indictment of our power structure as exceedingly classist and close-minded. Nowhere are conformity and groupthink encouraged more than in the power seminaries of the Ivy League. This has caused a severe creativity shortage in our ruling class, and it is hastening our downfall.

Crisis of Creativity

America is a nation borne of immigrant diversity. This breadth of races, experiences and skills has cultivated a people whose ability to generate new ideas is unparalleled in human history. Unfortunately that diversity of thought is not reflected in our government.

More Congress people are attorneys by trade than any other profession. The contest isn't even close. The problem though is not the presence of lawyers per se. The issue is a large majority of Congress members coming from any one discipline. Members of any professional grouping will share similar educations and skill sets. Furthermore, a confluence of one profession often leads to career-based legislative protectionism, whereby the interests of the people within that field are protected from legal inconvenience.

A preponderance of any profession in a legislative body will also tend to dominate the conversation and stifle creativity. Creativity is the engine of human progress, and any legislative body should be a reminder of this maxim.

False Advertising

We accept our politicians' obvious failings because our elections only allow for two options in the voting booth: One candidate who we can stomach, and one who we cannot. This binds us so strongly to the "acceptable" candidate that we continue to support him or her even when they abandon their ideological principles.

So deep is our collective partisan sycophancy that we have consistently ignored overt presidential trespasses against their own stated party platforms. Democratic presidents do not consistently represent the ideals of their constituencies. The same is true of Republican presidents.

Barack Obama received an unprecedented amount of campaign donations from Wall Street. His administration also continuously used unmanned drones to kill foreign nationals and American citizens without trial. These are actions typically railed against by the Democratic voter faithful. He is still their darling.

George W. Bush presided over an increase in the national debt of 4.9 trillion dollars.[vi] He also initiated the Iraq War, costing thousands of military and civilian lives and untold riches. These actions do not a conservative archetype make. He is still their darling.

Bill Clinton enacted the Welfare Reform Act of 1996, removing thousands of families from the welfare rolls and placing a five-year limit on benefits. Clinton's support of this bill enraged many Democrats and had them predicting a flood of starving homeless in America's streets. He is still their darling.

George Herbert Walker Bush famously raised taxes via the 1990 Budget Enforcement Act, after stating at the Republican Convention "Read my lips, no new taxes." It was the definition of a campaign lie for the entire world to see. He is still their darling.

Time and time again, constituencies on the left and the right have been let down by their supposed leaders' compromised principles. The base voters are often taken for granted by each party because they are guaranteed votes. Once elected, the candidate can do as he or she pleases in order to maintain their power. The only danger for an ideologically wayward candidate is a primary challenge. However, once a candidate has amassed a substantial campaign surplus, such challenges usually prove fruitless.

The merits of any of the afore-mentioned policies notwithstanding, the presidents who Democrats and Republicans have chosen to represent their values have regularly betrayed them. Still, they continue to reap the benefits of traditional partisan support. As the committed subjects of Republican and Democratic presidents, we are powerless. The parties must be held to account by all, including their own supposed constituencies.

American Monarchy

Our blind allegiance to the tyrants is now leading us down a regressive path toward a mutant political monarchy. Today, holding a presidential surname qualifies as a leadership credential. DNA-sharing with a former president should not necessarily disqualify one from consideration. Nevertheless, we seem all too eager to assume that name recognition alone is a sufficient determinant of competence. Bad presidential reboots are becoming as common as bad movie reboots.

This is a result of a political culture that oversimplifies everything. Problems are oversimplified to accommodate oversimplified solutions. The same goes for our view of potential candidates. Rather than analyzing the depth of any candidate's knowledge of an issue, we look for a psychological quick fix in choosing allegiances.

Two Tyrants

First we look at party membership. Then we look for the name we recognize. This leads to a frightening advantage for those with familial ties in politics. Political inheritance is a dangerous game, and we must be vigilant against it.

A Debilitating Disease

Our willing complicity in the two-party charade has caused an epidemic of Terminal Incumbency in Washington. This is a condition by which party hackery eventually leads to a Congress member's timely death in office. Their demise is usually preceded by two to three decades of worsening symptoms that include "poor foresight", "chronic pointed-finger", and "bloated war-chest".

Congressional incumbent reelection over recent decades has hovered around 80%.[vii] Declining public conditions and poor approval ratings would suggest that this reelection rate is a major source of our woes. Nevertheless, incumbents continue to sail to electoral victory within the framework designed exclusively by (and for) the Democrats and Republicans.

Monopoly Men

In fairness, the US Congress is not populated solely by perverted convicts and senile geriatrics. It also boasts a growing number of out-of-touch rich people. In 2012, the US Congress passed an unfortunate milestone. The 113th Congress is the first in history that has a majority of members who are millionaires.[viii] This statement should terrify anyone who believes in a government of the people, by the people, for the people.

Many of the world's nations that are crippled by corruption can attest to the dangers of rule by economic elites. The financial gap between the ruling class and the citizenry breeds misunderstanding and poor policy-making. A government of millionaires cannot effectively govern a nation of our size with any real understanding of the issues we face. Granted, we all want tax breaks for car-elevator installation. That's just a basic human right. But when it comes to the concrete issues that shape our daily lives, they have no idea what we need.

Furthermore, the fact that more than half of our legislators are millionaires should be cause for concern on an ethical level. Current annual salary for a member of the US House or Senate is $174,000. This means that two conditions exist under which all of these Congress people acquired their wealth. Some were millionaires before they were elected. This implies that a seat in the halls of power can easily be purchased. The remaining Congress people became millionaires *while* serving in office. This situation would suggest illegal, or at the least unethical means of acquiring wealth. Using one's status as a politician to gain riches is all too common in America, and the statistics seem to indicate that it's only getting worse.

Fewer Parties, More Problems

Despite the obvious corruption and failure of our current politics, some argue that a two-party solution is still the best option for America. Respected columnist Zev Chafets has stated that the two party system is not the evil that some would suggest. He claims that living in a country (Israel) with over a dozen political parties offered him a less representative government than the US.[ix] Using this reasoning to support the two tyrants is fatally flawed. By applying the same logic one could conclude that fewer parties always equals a more representative government.

Therefore, if a two-party system is stable, then a one-party government must be absolute divinity. Evidence to the contrary abounds. Single-party rule is always a disaster. Mexico's Revolutionary Institutional Party ruled from 1929 to 2000.[x] This period was arguably one of the most violent and economically disastrous periods in all of Latin American history.

Similarly, Augusto Pinochet's decades-long military junta ruled Chile without opposition, resulting in the imprisonment and murder of untold numbers of political dissidents. Single-party regimes throughout the world have consistently been the poster-children for human atrocities and political oppression. Consolidation of power in the hands a few ruling elite is never a recipe for freedom or progress. Two powerful ruling parties with near-total control of any nation are only one small degree of separation from single-party rule, and total dictatorship.

Outliers

For all of our current failures, good candidates and good leaders do exist in American politics. Many Republican and Democratic politicians as individuals are well intentioned and capable. These are worthy politicians in spite of their party affiliation, not because of it. Unfortunately, the parties stifle the creativity and effectiveness of most of their own candidates.

Each party's metric for success becomes defeat of the political opposition. Rarely is the actual solution of a public problem the true measure of political aptitude. This leads the party leadership to advise candidates and elected officials to avoid risk at all costs. Any new idea not within the parameters of standard party principles is discouraged. This is especially true of non-incumbent candidates who are easily molded in the hopes of gaining a seat. What results is a very short political shelf life for most risk-favorable candidates.

Any potentially capable politicians are working within the previously designed political structure that they see before them. If that structure changes, most can and will adapt to their new surroundings. If they are indeed good leaders, they will flourish within their newfound ideological freedom.

The Wizard of Us

Resistance to our two-party dysfunction is everywhere. In September of 2014, A Gallup poll determined that 47% of Americans identify as independents, while a lesser 26% and 25% identify as Democrats and Republicans respectively. 47% is the highest percentage ever polled by Gallup of self-identified independents.[xi] Furthermore, A 2014 Reason-Rupe report states that half of all millennials do not trust either party.[xii]

An even more telling statistic was revealed in a 2014 Washington Post-ABC News voter satisfaction poll. For the first time in its history (over 25 years) the poll found that a majority of Americans disapproved of their own member of the US House of Representatives.[xiii] This is important because it highlights a new level of discontentment with Congress. Traditionally, Americans have seen Congress as unfavorable, but were satisfied with their own elected representative. Such a viewpoint led incumbents to enjoy easy reelection even if they were doing a sub-par job.

Taken together, these polls prove that Americans are starting to see the wizard for what he is: A half-witted megalomaniac peddling fear to gain power. An Independent or third party presidency is likely if the electoral system begins to reflect the will of the people. Some may see the 47% of independents as frustrated individuals. They are a much more powerful force than that. They are a majority, and the key to our future.

PARTY IDENTIFICATION OF AMERICAN VOTERS

★ *Gallop Poll / September 2014* ★

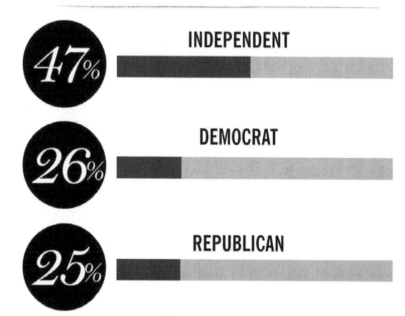

INDEPENDENT

47%

DEMOCRAT

26%

REPUBLICAN

25%

Strange Bedfellows

Dissatisfaction with the status quo is not limited to any ideological ism. The signs of political frustration come from all over the philosophical spectrum. From the left, the Occupy Wall Street movement has rallied around a cry of corporate manipulation and political corruption. The movement has vast numbers, and even more nominal supporters on the sidelines. What Occupy *doesn't* have is an end game.

From the right, the Tea Party movement is a result of the growing power of the federal government. Tea Partiers are fighting against overtaxing and irresponsible government spending practices. The Tea Party mission is more defined than that of their Occupy counterparts. The goal is to elect "Tea Party" candidates to office within the Republican Party via the party primary process. This tactic amounts to a pseudo third party campaign. While the Tea Party has had limited electoral success, they are still beholden to the Republican Party's dogma and leadership. The problems inherent in the party cannot be changed from within.

Both groups mistrust our current government stewards. They are both correct in many of their complaints. Corporations do have too much power and influence over our government. Also, the federal government spends more money than it has (See previous national debt discussion.), often on fraudulent and wasteful programs. Both problems are the fault of the tyrants.

Nevertheless, the system actually encourages that these two groups oppose each other, rather than fight against the structure causing the dysfunction. If the Occupy and Tea Party groups would focus their frustration on our voting process, they would both ultimately move closer to solving their respective policy grievances for good.

Third Party Pipe Dreams

Some frustrated voters support a third party. If our elections were just, this would be a reasonable means of balancing power. Unfortunately, third party advocates are often victims of their own egotistical idealism. They believe that better ideas will naturally lead to electoral success. However, the Republicans and Democrats did not gain their positions through superior solutions. Nor do they maintain them because of a firm grasp of policy issues. They hold our fate in their hands because we are all watching reality television instead of watching reality.

American political power is a direct result of a corrupted voting system and psychological manipulation. The most obvious proof of this is the lackluster results of the major third party movements of the 20th century. Many of these parties had substantial numbers and motivated voter bases. The most notable of these were the Reform Party, the Green Party and the

Libertarian Party. None of these parties were able to make any significant gains in congressional or presidential campaigns.

The current state of affairs dictates that third party candidates only serve to gift-wrap the election for whichever tyrant is most distasteful to the third party's supporters. Case in point, in 1992 Ross Perot's Reform Party presidential bid won the election for Bill Clinton. Similarly, in 2000 Green Party presidential candidate Ralph Nader handed the election to George W. Bush. These examples highlight just how frighteningly undemocratic our elections have become.

American voters have been clamoring for a change to our politics for decades. We have been searching for a transformational hero, grasping at anyone who sounds like they oppose the status quo. Look at the examples of Ross Perot, Jessie Ventura, Ralph Nader and Ron Paul. Unfortunately, no third party crusader can rise within the current political parameters.

Our politics have not changed for over a century, and will never do so if we continue to put our faith in loyalist insiders or powerless outsiders. Neither of these options can affect reform. Supporting any third party candidate for president within the current political confines is an exercise in the absurd. The Democratic and Republican parties are too deeply entrenched in our elections and our collective psyche to allow any third party to rise.

Two Tyrants

Independents' Day

Unlike third party voters, many Americans don't support *any* political party. Some don't vote at all, while others (independents) cast their vote based on candidate intangibles. Both of these approaches can be attempts at subversion. Neither is effective.

Those who choose not to vote do so either out of frustration or a lack of interest. The uninterested voter will likely never gain the motivation to be involved. The frustrated voter on the other hand is trying to make a statement with their non-vote. They are attempting to register their disgust with the lack of serviceable options on the ballot. Unfortunately, a non-vote only serves as a non-statement.

The only way to register contempt for a candidate is to vote *against* them. This is a difficult proposition in our current binary-leaning elections. Often, the only way to vote against one tyrant is to vote for the other one. And so goes the carrousel of American politics, round and round with no end in sight.

Independent voters are subjected to a biennial parade of candidates with whom they share little political common ground. Their votes usually end up largely based on gut feelings and perceptions of the candidate formed through media exposure. This approach strengthens our overlords' death-grip. It reduces an election to a series of photo opportunities and sound bites between two unsatisfactory candidates. What often results is a win by the candidate with the best cosmetic dentist, or fewest degrees of separation between themselves and Oprah Winfrey.

Furthermore, unaffiliated voters are at the whim of the party primary process. The majority of voters do not vote in primaries. Those who do vote in the primaries are often the most fervent party acolytes. The result is a general election candidate not fit for public consumption. It forces the general election voters to choose between two extremes. Like everyone else, un-affiliated voters get to choose between Candidate Bad and Candidate Worse in every general election. Independent voters in America are utterly voiceless.

Non-Partisan America

America's form of government is not a "two-party system." If it were, both parties would be official arms of the government, which they are not. Political parties in America are self-governed autonomous entities, completely independent of the government. They have no official connection to any government structure—federal, state, or municipal.

Political parties are not mentioned in the Declaration of Independence, the Constitution, or any other founding documents. Political parties in America (Republicans and Democrats included) have a less official connection to the US government than the local

Two Tyrants

PTA. They are merely a group of people who have pooled together because of shared political goals. The two dominant parties have convinced us that they are the rightful heirs to a political dynasty. Such an implication is political blasphemy.

Furthermore, Americans have already proven that two-party rule is not the only viable political option. Some of the largest cities in America hold non-partisan mayoral elections. Los Angeles, Dallas, Phoenix, Detroit and Seattle are but a few of the many major American cities to embrace non-partisan municipal elections.

Most of the Mayors who become elected to these posts are members of the Democratic or Republican parties. Most are politicians by trade, who have already been working their way through the party ranks in partisan races. Nevertheless, the existence of such a large number of non-partisan seats in major cities proves that non-partisan races are a perfectly acceptable way to maintain a stable and democratically elected government in America.

U.S. CITIES HOLDING NON-PARTISAN MAYORAL ELECTIONS

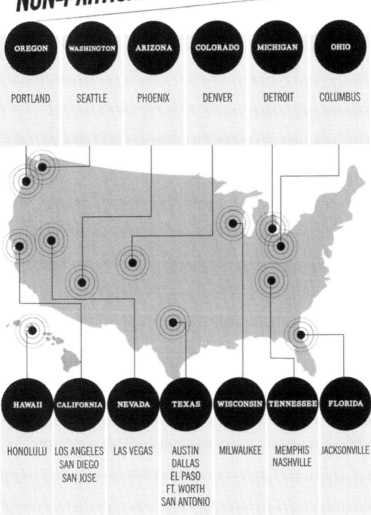

OREGON	WASHINGTON	ARIZONA	COLORADO	MICHIGAN	OHIO
PORTLAND	SEATTLE	PHOENIX	DENVER	DETROIT	COLUMBUS

HAWAII	CALIFORNIA	NEVADA	TEXAS	WISCONSIN	TENNESSEE	FLORIDA
HONOLULU	LOS ANGELES	LAS VEGAS	AUSTIN	MILWAUKEE	MEMPHIS	JACKSONVILLE
	SAN DIEGO		DALLAS		NASHVILLE	
	SAN JOSE		EL PASO			
			FT. WORTH			
			SAN ANTONIO			

Two Tyrants

In addition to the afore-mentioned mayorships, the entire legislature of the state of Nebraska is run as a non-partisan body. The Nebraska Legislature is the only unicameral non-partisan state legislature in the entire nation. Each legislative district in Nebraska holds an open non-partisan primary.[xiv] Despite the official non-partisan status of the legislature, most senators are either Republicans or Democrats. As in the case of the above mayorships, Nebraska legislators must operate within the current political reality, where a lack of Democratic or Republican affiliation is practically a death sentence, even in non-partisan races.

Non-partisan elections can and do happen in America. They are not a danger to our democracy. They are only a danger to those who fear progress.

The State of Louisiana Politics

The state of Louisiana holds non-partisan blanket primaries for all municipal and statewide offices. This type of primary sees all candidates run against each other in a primary regardless of party. The top two vote getters from the primary then run against one another in the general election. Even if both candidates are from the same party, they still face one another in the general election.[xv]

This election format weakens the undue influence of the two parties. Although such elections are preferable to what is in place in most other states, they are far from perfect. One of the major disadvantages of such a system is that it can lead to electoral victories by candidates with a small plurality of votes.

For example, in an open primary with four liberals and two conservatives, vote splitting between the four liberals could yield the two conservatives as top vote getters. Even if more people voted for liberal candidates in the primary, they could end up with two conservative general election candidates. Such discrepancies could be avoided by adding a simple weighting system to the voting process, which is discussed in Chapter III.

Moving On

We have recreated the same situation that the first Europeans on this soil were fleeing. The corrupt church (Republicans) wants to control our morality. The corrupt king (Democrats) wants to control our money. However, we don't need a revolution. We need reform. There is nothing inherently wrong with our economic system or our political system.

We have been misled by the Republican and Democratic conglomerates to believe that they are our only choices, but the US Constitution tells us otherwise. This country was built by radical revolutionaries, from the founding fathers to the founders of Apple. But we've entrusted their brilliant creation to a succession of increasingly unimaginative empty suits (and pantsuits). We are all the intellectual descendants of our radical revolutionary predecessors, and we bear the burden of protecting their vision. They never intended for us to live under a carbon copy presidency or a think-nothing Congress.

Support for these two power-drunk malcontents is support for elitism, corruption, and aristocratic political incumbency. This is not a moral indictment of any individual voter, but a statement about the political oppression we all face. Most support this system completely unwittingly, as true believers in the their candidate and their party.

Our inability as American brothers and sisters to separate our decision-making from our political affiliation has become a grave psychological disorder. The tyrants' lies and corruption have predicated the downfall of the most free and powerful civilization in human history.

The current political structure is the precursor to collapse. The only question now is what that collapse will entail. Will the entire structure crumble and whither away to rubble, or will we reform and renovate from within? The universe is bellowing from every direction that it's time to move forward. Our job is to act.

Chapter II

Origins

II

The Roots

Recognizing the cause of our unfortunate political circumstance is the first step toward repairing it. Facing the mistakes of the past can open the door the solutions of the future. We must examine how we became the unwitting torchbearers of lowbrow political manipulation and ideological peasantry. Political parties did not always hold the influence in our government that they do today.

George Washington was not a member of any political party throughout his entire presidency. In fact, during his presidential farewell address Washington warned his compatriots of the failings of political parties with the following declaration:

> The alternate domination of one faction over another, sharpened by the spirit of revenge

> natural to party dissension, which in different ages & countries has perpetrated the most horrid enormities, is itself a frightful despotism. But this leads at length to a more formal and permanent despotism. The disorders & miseries, which result, gradually incline the minds of men to seek security & repose in the absolute power of an Individual: and sooner or later the chief of some prevailing faction more able or more fortunate than his competitors, turns this disposition to the purposes of his own elevation, on the ruins of Public Liberty.[xvi]

This statement is an abject rejection of political parties as the arbiters of governmental policy. Nevertheless, political parties have indeed become a rational part of American political life. However, the existence of political parties need not be synonymous with uncontested domination by two omnipresent political ogres.

In the Beginning

Our two primary ideological tribes evolved from two very defined founding factions: The Federalists and the Anti-Federalists. The Federalists (Washington, Madison and Hamilton) were in favor of a more robust, powerful federal apparatus to hold our young union together. The Anti-Federalists (Patrick Henry, George Clinton, Roger Sherman) were concerned with the ability of a strong federal government to overwhelm the semi-sovereign authority of the states.

The echoes of Federalist and Anti-Federalist arguments can still be heard in our modern left vs. right arguments. These two competing philosophies have continued to dominate the political discourse for most of our history. They have become part of our national political identity.

Because the federal power vs. state power debate was such an influential part of our initial development, it will always be ingrained in our political culture. Unfortunately, this important discussion has become inextricably linked to the Republican and Democratic parties. This debate can and should occur completely independent of the parties. Linking the state vs. federal debate to the tyrants is wholly inappropriate, as not even the parties themselves maintain fidelity to their supposed side of the argument.

Power Players

Once the Democrats and Republicans gained a solid foothold in our political life, complex political scaffolding developed around them to protect their positions. Some of the structure was created deliberately and some was incidental. They have become so connected to our thoughts about politics that it's not unusual to hear voters suggesting that Jesus himself would have supported the policies of one party or another.

The government, party surrogates, the media, and even our own psychology reinforce this dangerous lie on a daily basis. The key to breaking free of the tyrants' mind control lays in understanding how it works. What has been done can be undone, but only if we recognize that we are responsible for freeing our own minds.

Government's Role in the Two-Party Myth

Government structures at all levels perpetuate two-party domination through a systematic legitimization campaign. The Republican and Democratic parties have uncontested dominion over every level of our government. They abuse this power daily to reinforce their own influence. They use the tools of government to imply their own legitimacy and deny access to all comers. They do so by the following means:

Restrictive Ballot Access: Ballot access refers to the ease or difficulty with which a candidate can get their name included on an election ballot. The United States has some of the most restrictive ballot access laws in the world. As such, it is a daunting proposition for any Independent or third party candidate to get on the ballot for a congressional or presidential bid.

The Democratic and Republican establishments whole-heartedly support the restrictive nature of ballot access in America because it secures their power. Each state makes its own laws regarding ballot access. This includes ballot access laws for federal offices such as Congress and president.

Unfortunately, most ballot access laws rely heavily on a combination of valid petition signatures, and a minimum vote percentage of totals from the prior election. America's ballot access laws create the perfect environment for the two tyrants to maintain their illegitimate stranglehold on our government.

Government Support for Party Primaries: The primary presidential and congressional election process for the two parties varies slightly by state. Nevertheless, it is always a masterstroke of political theatre, and we all have front row seats. Local government's role in funding and facilitating party primaries implies that these primaries are actual government elections. They are not. They are elections of an independent organization's preferred candidate.

Because the two parties are in complete control of every level of government, they appear to be one in the same. The primary election process in America leads voters to believe that Republican and Democratic primaries are the first step in the American government's election process. This is an unforgivable untruth.

Under the current primary framework, each party chooses their candidate. The rest of us then get to choose which of them will offer us a less painful demise. We marvel at one of the two over-groomed simpletons before us, and choose to ignore their magnificent sameness. This is not choice. This is not democracy. It is indentured political servitude, from which we must earn our freedom.

Much has been written of America's penchant for "exporting democracy". An election format as democratically repressive as ours would quickly draw the ire of Congress if it were operating in another country. The Senate would surely authorize B52s to drop all the democracy in our arsenal on said country in the hopes of liberating it from such an obviously oppressive regime.

General Election Format Favoring Two Parties: The manner in which we conduct our general elections inherently favors domination of two parties. In Jeffrey D. Sachs' 2011 book The Price of Civilization, he explained

> The main reason for America's majoritarian character is the electoral system for Congress. Members of Congress are elected in single-member districts according to the "first-past-the-post" (FPTP) principle, meaning that the

> candidate with the plurality of votes is the winner of the congressional seat. The losing party or parties win no representation at all. The first-past-the-post election tends to produce a small number of major parties, perhaps just two, a principle known in political science as Duverger's Law. Smaller parties are trampled in first-past-the-post elections.[xvii]

In addition to our FPTP elections, the fact that our general elections are almost always comprised of one Republican and one Democrat acculturates voters to the concept of two-party dominance. We believe from our first electoral experiences that one Republican plus one Democrat equals a free and fair election.

Partisan Elections: When we enter the voting booth, Americans tend to look for a (D) or an (R) next to the candidate name. This is a result of lifelong indoctrination by the tyrants and their agents. We see this as the best determinant of the candidates' beliefs and future actions. This exercise offers a false sense of accomplishment. Party affiliation is no indicator of competence, honesty, or ideological fidelity. Yet the local, state and federal governments all print party affiliation next to a candidate's name on voting ballots. This is done as a legitimizing tactic for the Democratic and Republican candidates. It also serves to delegitimize in the minds of voters any candidates not of the elephantine or equine persuasion.

No government entity should endorse, nor discount the legitimacy of *any* political party. Government neutrality is the ideal. So sacred is the act of voting in America that it is done in secret. This is to protect the voter against any undue influence or retribution from other stakeholders. Nevertheless, the government itself is imposing undue influence on the voter by identifying party affiliation on the ballot. Such is not the responsibility of the government. The burden of educating voters on candidate platforms lays with the candidate him or herself.

This seemingly innocuous act implies that party identification is a valid predictor of future performance. The candidate's party affiliation is no more important than their favorite food, or favorite football team. It is simply an organization with which they identify. It has no tangible bearing on their abilities as legislator or executive.

A (D) or an (R) next to a candidate's name also implies organizational support. Organizational support was never intended by our founding fathers to be a litmus test for competent or moral leadership. On the contrary, our nation was founded partly based on an overt mistrust of large bureaucratic institutions with appetites for skullduggery. Nevertheless, as humans we seek comfort in perceived legitimacy, which partisan candidates use to their advantage.

Two Tyrants

Pseudo-Government's Role in the Two-Party Myth

"Pseudo-Government" refers to the Republican and Democratic parties and their election-adjacent functionaries. Both parties use every tool at their disposal to sell voters the lie of a two-party American government. Our government is to be guided by individual conscience and not tribal alliances. The tyrants tell us otherwise, and they have become frighteningly adept at blurring the lines between parties and government.

The Commission on Presidential Debates: The presidency of the United States of America is the most influential job on the planet. As such, determining the occupant of the Oval Office should be a sober and thorough affair. The current presidential debate process is a con-job, a corporate farce, and a masterpiece of wool pulling for the ages.

Since 1987, the Commission on Presidential Debates has coordinated all televised presidential and vice-presidential debates. According to the Commission's own website

> **The Commission on Presidential Debates (CPD) was established in 1987 to ensure that debates, as a permanent part of every general election, provide the best possible**

information to viewers and listeners. Its primary purpose is to sponsor and produce debates for the United States presidential and vice presidential candidates and to undertake research and educational activities relating to the debates. The organization, which is a nonprofit, nonpartisan, 501(c)(3) corporation, sponsored all the presidential debates in 1988, 1992, 1996, 2000, 2004, 2008, and 2012.[xviii]

Unfortunately, the above description of the CPD's activities does not give an accurate view of their mission. "Non-partisan" is not an apt description of their leadership. It probably falls somewhere between mega-partisan and galacto-partisan. It is an organization populated by Democrats and Republicans for the sole purpose of promoting the duopoly of the tyrants. A review CDP leadership shows the obvious hypocrisy of their self-described non-partisanship (See opposite page.).

PARTY AFFILIATION OF CPD LEADERSHIP

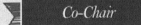

Co-Chair

FRANK J. FAHRENKOPF, JR.
Former Chair,
Republican National Committee

Co-Chair

MICHAEL D. McCURRY
Former Press Secretary,
Democratic President Bill Clinton

Executive Director

JANET H. BROWN
Former Press Secretary,
Republican Senator J. Danforth

Furthermore, the CPD Board of Directors is comprised of Republican and Democratic power brokers and their intellectual and media cohorts. The primary function of the CPD is to perpetuate the lie of our republic as a two-party creation. The Commission on Presidential Debates is the very definition of political collusion. Presidential debates in America will continue to be an illegitimate lie so long as the CPD is charged with their facilitation.[xix]

Consumer advocate and former Green Party presidential candidate Ralph Nader consistently complained that the Commission on Presidential Debates was an organization tasked primarily with silencing outside voices.[xx] Nader is hardly the only politico to decry the disingenuous ends of the CPD. Former Nixon aide and Reform Party presidential candidate Pat Buchanan also complained of the CPD's exclusionary tactics.[xxi] Any organization that can bring that level of agreement between Ralph Nader and Pat Buchanan may very well be ushering in the end of days.

❝❝ THE COMMISSION ON PRESIDENTIAL DEBATES IS A PRIVATE CORPORATION CREATED IN 1987 BY THE DEMOCRATIC AND REPUBLICAN PARTIES TO **SEIZE COMPLETE CONTROL OVER THE PRESIDENTIAL DEBATE PROCESS.** ITS PRINCIPAL OBJECTIVES ARE TO EXCLUDE COMPETITORS FROM THIRD PARTIES OR INDEPENDENT CANDIDACIES, AND TO CONTROL THE NUMBER AND FORMATS OF DEBATES. **❞❞**

Ralph Nader,
Green Party Presidential Candidate, 2004

❝❝ I SHOULD BE INCLUDED IN THE PRESIDENTIAL DEBATE BECAUSE **I'M THE REPRESENTATIVE OF A RECOGNIZED PARTY—** ONE OF THREE: REPUBLICANS, DEMOCRATS AND REFORM. THE OTHER TWO PARTIES ARE ENGAGED IN A CONSPIRACY, BASICALLY TO DENY ME ACCESS TO THE DEBATE THAT IS GOING TO DECIDE THE ELECTION AND THE PRESIDENCY OF THE UNITED STATES... **THE AMERICAN PEOPLE ARE BEING DENIED THE RIGHT TO SEE AND HEAR A CANDIDATE THEY ARE PAYING FOR.❞❞**

Patrick Buchanan,
Reform Party Presidential Candidate, 2000

Republican and Democratic National Committees: The Democratic and Republican national committees are two of the most powerful organizations on earth. Each committee is made up of political activists and politicians who elect a National Chair. The Chair's role is to lead the party's election efforts. It is the job of the Chair to ensure that incumbent politicians retain their seats, and that non-incumbents win contested seats nation-wide.

Each committee chair is paid over $100,000 a year. Aside from the pay, they enjoy tremendous perks, including access to and influence over the most powerful people in America. National committee chairs have more interest in winning the daily public relations battle than in actually fixing pervasive policy problems.

Most Republican and Democratic Committee Chairs have been exceptional at keeping the lie machine well oiled and fully functioning. Ponder for a moment all the buzzwords used by Democratic and Republican presidential candidates over the past twenty-five years. "Education, Middle Class, Security, Opportunity and Freedom" are but a few. How many of those issues have improved in the past two and a half decades?

America's education continues to worsen. The middle class has shrunk. We are less secure, and we have less opportunity than we did 25 years ago. Nonetheless, every election season both national committees seem to convince us that their new model is our savior incarnate. They perform a flawless, Men In Black style memory-purge on three hundred million of us every election year and the whole process begins again.

Party-Controlled Presidential Primaries: The party primary process is protracted one, often lasting for months. This means that whichever states hold primaries or caucuses earlier have a greater influence over voters in the states that vote later in the process. Is there any logical reason why states such as Iowa and New Hampshire have such a disproportionate influence over the leadership of the entire nation?

The extended primary season also benefits both parties in terms of media coverage. Each primary and caucus tends to function as its own electoral Super Bowl, so to speak. Each primary day throughout the season comes with a traveling circus of journalists and the like, covering the dog and pony show.

The primary season functions as a months-long infomercial for both parties. Furthermore, the beginning stages of the primary season often sees upwards of six or seven candidates from each party. This leads us to believe that we have a diverse pool of candidates from which to choose our president. Unfortunately, most of the candidates in each party's primary are all shades of the same color (mostly beige).

Media's Role in the Two-Party Myth

The American media is the greatest ally of both the Republicans and the Democrats. The vast majority of media personalities have chosen their team, and it's easy to match personality with party. From the political punditry on 24-hour news to basic cable satirists to pop tart starlets --every corner of our media is pushing the ideological smack of one side or the other. They convince us to fight against the "other" within the current political confines. They *should* be convincing us to fight against the structure that keeps both sides fat, rich and powerful.

Political Punditry: Rush Limbaugh, Rachel Maddow and their ilk are political tools (pun intended) of the tyrants. They are the archetypes of a creature we see on a daily basis. They take their marching orders from their respective sides, and laugh all the way to the bank. They spin the lie of a tangible difference between the two parties. Although political media personalities are the most obvious of targets, Democratic and Republican influence goes well beyond televised blowhard shouting-matches.

News Coverage: The tyrants control the American news media. As unofficial party functionaries, news organizations proselytize with nearly every report. Some of their propaganda is overt and some is covert. On the overt side, Fox News and MSNBC spend the vast amount of their airtime preaching to the choir. One would think they receive a royalty payment for every "that's right" a viewer screams at the television set.

Most newspapers also have a relatively well-known slant to their news coverage as well as their editorial pages. Think New York Times vs. Wall Street Journal. While the political differences in newspapers may not be as explicit in the US as in places like Britain, the differences are definitely discernible.

On the covert side, story selection and narrative framing are the most common tools of the trade. It is impossible to report news with finite impartiality. To imply otherwise is intellectually juvenile. News services offer an infinite range of stories on a daily basis. News producers and editors naturally choose to highlight the stories that they feel are most important. As such, their own prejudices and political leanings will always influence their choices.

Broadcast news and newspapers continually promote an agenda whether they admit it or not. Many times they do so with no awareness of their own participation in the brainwashing process. This further highlights the extent of the tyrants' power over our psychology.

Additionally, major networks cover Republican and Democratic political theater ad nauseam. There is no network coverage for any other party's news conferences, conventions or primary elections. The coverage of America's political goings-on and lack thereof reinforces public perceptions of two-party legitimacy.

Entertainment-Political Complex: Those in the entertainment industry use their own bully pulpit to promote the candidates of their choice, and ridicule the opposition. It is their right to do so. Unfortunately, the greater result of their actions is the legitimization of one of the two parties. Any public sanctioning of one party is an endorsement of the system that keeps them both in power.

Another psychological impact of the entertainment-political complex is the rise of the politician-as-celebrity mentality. If every politician has only one ideological opponent, pop-culture fluency is more likely to be tantamount to policy issues. The politician must put as much importance on the hipness of their Instagram feed as the depth of their policy knowledge.

Propaganda Over Policy

According to the Merriam-Webster dictionary, propaganda is defined as "ideas or statements that are often false or exaggerated and that are spread in order to help a cause, a political leader, a government, etc."[xxii] As explained above, the government, the pseudo-government, and the media work in concert in one of the greatest propaganda machines of all time. They each have their role to play, and have done so almost flawlessly for decades. It is this apparatus that has convinced us all that the current political reality is our destiny. This is a lie. Their job is to maintain political power in perpetuity and we have all played right into their hands.

The greatest impact that propaganda has on a population is the effect on its psychology. Our current situation is no exception. The parties have created an elaborate framework around our society, convincing many of us that the two of them are the rightful heirs to American democracy. At some point we accepted this fate as reality and stopped questioning why. This is the point where our own minds began to reinforce the lie from within.

Psychology's Role in the Two-Party Myth

All of the afore-mentioned players in the tyrants' game of bait and switch contribute to our national illness. At some point, our own minds pick up the reigns and finish the job that the two parties started. We argue, justify and exasperate our way to party loyalty, and fight tooth and nail to protect our side's position.

Dual Philosophies: The development of two ideological poles in our political history has led us to our current psycho-political crossroads. As described above, the two parties grew out of a singular issue in post-revolutionary America. That philosophical battle became even more intense leading up to and during the Civil War. The trauma of the war and the role of the states rights vs. federal mandate argument further cemented this philosophical chasm. The next 100 years of political history only widened the gap between the two parties. Meanwhile, each side continued to shore up their foothold in American political life. By the middle of the 20th century Democrats and Republicans completely overwhelmed our national political discussion.

Choosing one tyrant or the other causes us to make intellectual concessions for our own side's imperfections. It is much easier to highlight the opposition's failings than to be self-critical. Therefore the current paradigm encourages a laser-like focus on the enemy's incompetence and corruption, and a blind eye to our own side's transgressions.

In 2013, Joseph Burgo penned an article for The Atlantic entitled "The Emotional Psychology of A Two-Party System." Burgo noted that an inherently human defense mechanism hinders compromise because we tend to completely support our own point of view and completely reject that of the opposition. In referencing the work of neurologist Robert Burton, Burgo wrote:

> ...ambiguity or confusion is so difficult for many of us to bear that we instead retreat from it into a feeling of certainty, believing we know something without any doubts, even when we

actually don't and often can't know. Those of us who have trouble with such discomfort often resort to black-and-white thinking instead. Rather than feeling uncertain or ambivalent, struggling with areas of gray, we reduce that complexity to either/or.

We may define one idea or point of view as bad (black) and reject it, aligning ourselves with the good (white) perspective. Feelings of anger and self-righteousness often accompany this process, bolstering our conviction that we are in the right and the other side in the wrong. Hatred for the rejected point of view keeps ambiguity and uncomfortable complexity from re-entering the field.

Black-and-white thinking reflects the psychological process known as splitting. When we feel unable to tolerate the tension aroused by complexity, we "resolve" that complexity by splitting it into two simplified and opposing parts, usually aligning ourselves with one of them and rejecting the other. As a result, we may feel a sort of comfort in believing we know something with absolute certainty; at the same time, we've over-simplified a complex issue.[xxiii]

Political Reality vs. Tangible Reality: In his groundbreaking 1922 book Public Opinion, Pulitzer

Prize winning journalist Walter Lippman wrote, "For the most part, we do not first see, and then define, we define first, and then see. In the great blooming, buzzing confusion of the outer world we pick out what our culture has already defined for us and we tend to perceive that which we have picked out in the form stereotyped for us by our culture."[xxiv]

Lippman highlighted the nature of stereotypes in our politics. He asserted that the complexity of our reality, including our politics, lends itself to psychological "quick-fixes" in the minds of voters. This tendency to simplify the convoluted shapes the politics in any democracy. Unfortunately, it has led us to seek comfort in the familiarity of the two dominant parties in our country, to the detriment of our policymaking.

Illusion of Choice: Free will separates human beings from all the other beasts on earth. It is the one inexorable desire that pushes mankind forward. Understanding this, the tyrants have engineered a voting system that offers the false promise of self-determination. In a single-party state, such as China, the Communist Party controls all. The people have no choice in the matter, and they know it. At least their rulers are honest about their dictatorship.

Those in charge of America suggest that we have complete dominion over whom we elect. Nevertheless, voters are summarily stripped of any decision-making power through the primary and general election process.

Two Tyrants

What often remains are the most over-coached and under-prepared candidates money can buy. The illusion of choice keeps us content in our squalor.

The Next Step

The Republican and Democratic parties believe that together they have a birthright to make our destiny in their own image. To date, we have all accepted this assumption without question. But the time has come for the new to challenge the established. Our exclusionary election process has led to a political caste system, with the tyrants on top, and everyone else in the realm of the untouchables.

Democratic and Republican ascent to power is a result of historical circumstance. Their staying power is a product of sustained psychological abuse. No political party on earth deserves over one and a half centuries of uninterrupted governance. The inherent fallibility of humans is reflected in the fallibility of our political parties. They've managed to maintain their power by infecting every facet of our society with political smoke and mirrors.

The only way to dismantle this mind-control apparatus is through election reform. The path to said reform runs directly through the voting booth. Our perceptions may be skewed, but our hands are not shackled. We still have the power of our vote, and the blessed responsibility it bestows upon us. Policy differences aside, we must come together to rescue our halls of power from the poison within.

Chapter III

Roadmap

III

The Way To Liberation

The American government no longer reflects the values of its people. It has become a model of institutionalized political prostitution. Our corrupted elections structure politely discourages politicians from biting the hand that feeds their offshore bank accounts. It is not the natural tendency of any tyrant to remove him or herself from power, but we have the numbers to act as our own liberators. The righteousness of our votes can restore true choice to American elections.

Just as the two parties have used election laws to consolidate their power, we can use the same laws to diminish it. The Democratic and Republican grip on our government is firm. Nevertheless it can be broken with strategic attention to a few key pressure points. The goal of these reforms should be the restoration of electoral populism. Rolling back our repressive election practices will open the door for a wider array of candidates to challenge the traditional powers.

Hurdles

Keeping us from taking that first step is a chorus of naysayers, rife with apocalyptic predictions of lawlessness and destruction. Such warnings should be ignored, as substantive change is always met with fear and hatred. The loudest protestations against progressive electoral reforms come from two primary groups.

The first group consists of those who fear the unknown. They are comfortable with the status quo and for them change is always uncomfortable. There is nothing inherently sinister about their discomfort, but it is counterproductive nonetheless.

The second group includes the power brokers who stand to lose their influence. This includes a significant number of politicians and those who surround them. Many of them are more skilled at influencing politics than policy, so a systemic shakeup would be a threat to their way of life. Survival is the strongest instinct of the human condition, and political survival is no different.

However, major electoral reform is not to be feared, as it is a vital part of America's political legacy. A number of institutional electoral changes have occurred throughout the past two and a half centuries, with successful results. In fact, most of the election reforms in our history have resulted in immeasurable expansions of freedom. Such reforms have always required great courage, and often led to great leaps in social progress.

America's Election Reform Record

Examples of massive shifts in voting policy are easy to find. In the 19th century, voting rights were extended to non-property-owners and black males. At the time, opponents of these expansions warned that they would lead to bedlam. Democrats argued strenuously against giving freed male slaves the right to vote, citing their high illiteracy rates as evidence that they would be swayed by false promises and bribery[xxv] (Democratic Party racial activism at its finest). Thankfully, the Congress of the day had the wherewithal to pass the 15th amendment and President Grant the fortitude to sign it into law. But this was in fact a step into the unknown.

In the 20th century, the right to vote was expanded to include women. In the 1910's, The National Association Opposed to Women Suffrage produced a pamphlet outlining the reasons why giving women the right to vote was a dangerous proposition. One of the reasons offered was "... it is unwise to risk the good we already have for the evil that may occur."[xxvi] In other words "if it ain't broke for me, don't fix it." Similarly, many claim that our two-party tradition is the only thing keeping us from complete anarchy. In this context, the word "many" is to be defined as Republicans and Democrats.

Thus far in the 21st century, no major national ballot access or voting format reforms have been enacted. Any substantive election reform bills typically fall on deaf congressional ears. Such is the case with most radical reforms proposed at the federal level. This unique moment in history offers us the perfect environment to demand, and achieve major electoral reform. It only requires that we become active in choosing the people who make decisions on our behalf.

The Path to Passage

Thankfully, the framers of the Constitution provided us with a tool for defending ourselves against electoral subjugation. Article four section one states that the authority to regulate time, place and manner of federal elections is up to each individual state, unless Congress legislates otherwise.[xxvii] This means that each state has the power to dictate the terms of congressional and presidential elections within their borders. The ability pass election reforms and drastically overhaul our government lies in the hands of each individual state.

Passing legislation at the state level is easier than at the federal level. Congress people and presidents are much more susceptible to the influence of large donors than their state counterparts. As a result, state legislators and governors enjoy more freedom to address and legislate on controversial topics (Legalized weed, anyone?).

The average citizen also has closer ties to their state legislators than they do to their Congress people. Grassroots organizing always starts at the local level, so the footprint of such a lobby at the state is much larger than it is in Washington. It is a more lucrative pursuit to advocate for common-sense election reform at the Statehouse than at the US Capitol.

The Reform Cocktail

The reform proposals that follow are intended to free us from our political masters. They are general guidelines, suggesting the types of reforms that can liberate our politics. Because of the variations in current state laws, local tuning of legislation is key. Nevertheless, passing some form of this legislation will greatly reduce the undue influence of the Democratic and Republican parties, giving voters more power over their own political destinies.

1. Uniform reductions in ballot access requirements for all state and federal elections.

For all state and federal elections, the first four candidates to procure valid petition signatures from five percent of the electorate may appear on the primary ballot. In the case of greater than four eligible submissions, the four nominees with the most valid petition signatures are to qualify.

America's hyper-stringent ballot access laws send a strong message to the average American: Your participation as candidate is neither wanted nor needed. Those with vast funds and organizational resources are currently treated as more deserving of nomination than John or Jane Q. Public. This is an inherently un-American dynamic, as it limits individual opportunity. Reducing the burden of ballot access laws for all candidates is integral to any worthwhile election reform plan.

Ballot access reform will finally put Independent and third party candidates on equal footing with Republicans and Democrats. As a result, citizen legislators will have as much opportunity to serve as professional politicians. This paradigm shift can only be healthy for our politics.

2. Publicly funded party primaries to be replaced by publicly funded non-partisan open primaries.

The primary election is to be a weighted election. Voters will rank their favored candidates from 1 to 4. A "1" holds more weight than a "2" and so forth. The top two ranking candidates from the primary move on to the two-person general election.

Government involvement in any internal party nominations is inappropriate and unfair. The government should be responsible for conducting open elections from start to finish. As such, an open primary for every office should be under the purview of the government. Primaries should serve as a way to weed out undesirables and allow the cream to rise to the top.

A non-partisan primary reduces the influence of preconceived notions. Such a primary system will also remove the blurred lines between party and government. The weighting system will ensure that the two winners continuing on to the general election truly reflect the political values of the electorate.

3. General elections to consist of runoff between two top candidates from weighted open primary.

Once past the primary challenge, the two top candidates will face each other in the general election. Party affiliation will have no bearing on general election participation. Should the voters choose two candidates of similar ideology, so be it.

The current general election process is the ineffective offspring of a broken primary process and unfair party influence. Allowing the two parties to dictate that they are the only real choices in any general election is a travesty. General election reform is a natural progression on the heels of the above primary reforms.

The outcome of such an election will be a winning candidate divergent from current candidates in two ways. Firstly, he or she will have had an easier road to candidate eligibility due to ballot access reform. Secondly, he or she will have gone through a more rigorous vetting process by voters due to increased competition for votes. This is a direct result of reforms that require a candidate to defend and promote their own ideas, rather than those of their party.

4. All state and federal general elections including presidential elections to be strictly non-partisan.

Regardless of whether any candidate receives more than 50% of votes in the primary, the top two candidates will always proceed to the general election. This will ensure that every voter has the opportunity to express the totality of their political preferences in both the primary and general elections.

State and federal elections should never be partisan endeavors. They only serve to hand every election to a Democrat or Republican without merit. Most importantly, the president of one of the most intellectually diverse cultures in human history should reflect those broad intellectual horizons. Government sanctioning of partisanship encourages a herd mentality amongst voters and erodes candidate quality.

The conversion from partisan to non-partisan elections will have both psychological and tangible repercussions. Mentally, voters will feel less pressure to choose a candidate by process of elimination. Votes will go to individuals, rather than parties. This means that candidates will have more of a responsibility to express ideas, rather than allegiances. Such changes will make for more intellectually robust campaigns.

Broad Results of Reform

The above simple reform plan offers a number of advantages over the current piecemeal process. Both sides of the equation will be improved. Candidates will be required to have a better handle on the issues due to challenges from multiple angles. This will yield more thoughtful policymaking, and allow candidates more ideological freedom as a base from which to legislate.

Voters will also have more responsibility for understanding candidates' positions, rather than simply their party identification. An informed electorate is key to any strong democracy. The above reforms will foster such an electorate.

Under the current system, panels of Republicans and Democrats make redistricting deals with each other in order to secure their own political safety. Redistricting has led to a level of incumbent job security that is anathema to progress. Reducing the influence of the parties by reducing their numbers will minimize the negative impacts of gerrymandering.

Reform may also result in increased voter turnout. A reformed system will show potential voters a marked difference in the quality of debate and eventual improvements in policy. Perceptions will thus change, encouraging increased participation in the democratic process.

Strategy for Passage

As previously discussed, 47% of Americans identify themselves politically as independents. This majority has the ability, if not the responsibility to assert its political independence. Coordination amongst reformist voters is the key to passing election reform.

Affecting change with the current crop of politicians is an uphill battle, as most are beneficiaries of the rigged system. Some may support the necessary measures, but most will initially cave to party pressure (insert jellyfish reference here). A coordinated voter revolt is the only way to accomplish the above legislative goals. The most powerful tool we have is our vote, and those who identify as independents are a voting block large enough to deny the tyrants the power they've enjoyed to this point.

The Revolving Door

In running for elective office, every politician enters into an implied contract with voters. He or she asks for the support of the constituency. In return, they agree to uphold promises made during the campaign. Though it would be unreasonable to expect a politician to keep every promise, one pledge made by every state and federal elected official should be unbreakable. The oath of office sworn by nearly all public officials in America requires office-holders to support, protect and defend the Constitution and government of the United States of America and their state.

By accepting the corrupt influence of the two tyrants, a politician breaks their solemn promise to the voters. Rather than defending the Constitution and government, they are allowing two political crime families to usurp constitutional intent. Therefore, any politician continuing to support two-party domination must be removed.

To pass electoral reform, the right legislators must be in place at the state level. Our job as disaffected voters is to provide some with motivation and others with walking papers. Most local and state politicians believe that party support offers the only path to electoral victory. To some extent, this is true. However, by using the negative power of our votes, we can show any candidate that our stick is bigger than their party's carrot.

The key to such a strategy is an amended social contract between voters. If we agree as a democratic collective that any politician who supports the current election protocols is unworthy, then the system can be changed. A strategy of support for the opposition of any non-reformist candidate is the most effective way to lobby for change.

Fear of defeat is the most motivating factor for almost any politician. Most state House elections occur every two years. For most state Senates and governorships it happens every four years. The following simple strategy, known as "The Revolving Door", can and will yield substantial results if voters are unified.

1. Identify state legislators and governors who will advocate and vote for the afore-mentioned reforms.

Those legislators and governors are to be supported. "Supported" means financially, electorally, and otherwise. Any legal means of electing pro-reform candidates should be explored.

2. The next election cycle is to be a referendum on success or failure of the reform bills during the previous legislative session.

Any incumbent who did not support and vote for major electoral reforms is to be rejected in both primary and general elections in favor of ANY deserving opponent. If the incumbent and the challenger are both non-reformists, the challenger is *always* to be supported. This revolving door strategy will ensure that any incumbent with the opportunity to support reforms will do so, if for no other reason than to maintain their substantial mortgage payments.

3. Repeat process until a legislative majority ensures passage of reforms.

Refusal to vote, legal action, and civil disobedience are all means of accomplishing the same end goal. However, the revolving door utilizes the electorate's greatest strength (numbers) and the politician's greatest weakness (fear of removal) more effectively.

USING THE NEGATIVE POWER OF OUR VOTES

Identify pro-election reform candidates. Vote for or against candidates based on this metric.

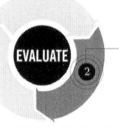

Assess legislator actions regarding election reform bills. Vote for or against candidates based on this metric.

Repeat process until legislative majority ensures passage of election reform bills.

Two Tyrants

The legislative process dictates that election laws are initiated in state House and Senate committees before being brought to the full chamber for a floor vote. Therefore, the above strategy should first be aimed at the committee Chair and committee members of both houses who will have the power to introduce and pass the bills in committee. Once the reform bills are brought to a floor vote, the strategy will be applied to all House and Senate members based on their votes.

State legislators and governors around the nation must be put on notice: Election reform is the most important issue on their docket. Obviously a matter as important as this should take precedence over any number of trivialities dealt with regularly by legislators. Not that naming an official state amoeba isn't of the utmost importance, but perhaps it can wait until the next legislative session.

Not only can we all speak with our votes, but also with our wallets. Those candidates in state races who support reforms can and should be monetarily supported from every corner of the republic. If the campaign finance laws are too permissive, we should use that to our advantage. After all, corporations may be people, but so are people (For now.). Everyone should donate and encourage donations to any state legislator or governor who supports reforms.

Any grassroots organization already operating is a resource for voter coordination. Social media is one of the most efficient means of highlighting candidate positions and potential alternative candidate campaigns; so in-state coordinators must utilize it to the utmost. Every state is unique, which means that decisions on organizing voter activism must be managed by local hands.

Incumbents and challengers are to be measured by a simple litmus test: Anyone voting for major electoral reform is to be supported. Anyone not doing so is to be removed by voter mandate. It is the responsibility of in-state activists to educate voters on which candidates are pro-reform and which are anti-reform. Until satisfactory electoral change is realized, these reforms are the most important issue by which any candidate is to be measured.

Defectors

Although a majority of Americans identify as independents, this is not a geographically universal statistic. The numbers vary by state and community. Some areas are in fact majority Republican and others are majority Democratic. Thus, independents alone cannot accomplish the overthrow of the tyrants. We need the help of current Democratic and Republican voters to participate in the movement.

These voters must understand that the goal is an improvement of our policies and *not* the destruction of their party. More intellectually competitive elections can only serve to improve the quality of candidates from any party. Accurate polls of party member satisfaction are hard to come by. Nevertheless, the mood in the country is one of frustration, and members of both parties are likely no exception. As mentioned previously, the Occupy and Tea Party movements offer at least circumstantial evidence of this dissatisfaction.

We must band together across ideological lines and recognize that the current election format will never yield the highest quality candidates. If Republican and Democratic voters want the best for their parties, then they should support election reform. Doing so will force their candidates to be more prepared leaders.

Democratic candidates only ever face Republican opposition and vice versa. This encourages both sides to repeat the same arguments every election cycle, with little reflection. When outside ideas and perspectives are introduced everyone will be forced to evaluate their own ideas on a new intellectual plane. Such a process offers great new possibilities for creativity and innovation in policymaking.

Advantages of Passage at State Level

Accomplishing these changes on a state-by-state basis offers a number of benefits. Sweeping national change is often met with harsh opposition, and fraught with logistical and political challenges. A state-by-state approach diminishes many of the potential pitfalls of drastic social change. This is why so many radical changes have, and continue to begin at the state level, leading to tectonic societal shifts.

The civil rights movement began locally in southern states and spread to eventual national recognition and support. The gay marriage and marijuana legalization movements are following that same pattern, with state legislative action leading to open debates and a domino effect in both passage and public opinion. Grassroots movements always have an advantage over top-down mandates.

Major election reform on the state level will bring the debate to voters' home turf. This makes voters active participants in the legislative process. At the state level, drafting of reform legislation can be done with local culture, history and concerns in mind. This makes for more locally palatable legislation. It also gives voters the time they may need to digest the concept of change. Americans have proven to be more open to new things when given time to adjust to them.

Incremental state-by-state reform lays the foundation for a more sustainable long-term change. It prolongs the debate and into a continuous, years-long discussion. This allows for local adaptation of bills, and makes it easier to accept to those who may have fears. Proximity is the best reducer of fear and mistrust when it comes to social and political change of this scale.

This approach is not only easier than national reform, but it will offer better results. We must follow the examples of successful social movements of the past and present. Some states will likely fall quickly while others will take more time. The history and culture of each state is individual, and the shape that reform will take will also be influenced by the culture.

Risks Vs. Rewards

Some may consider the proposed voter strategy reckless or even dangerous. If successful, the voter revolt would likely see a number of state legislators and governors serve one term only to be sent packing the very next election. The fear being that there would be an experience deficit within the halls of state government. Good. Better we have an experience deficit at the state level than an accountability deficit at the federal level.

Furthermore, the length of time in elected office is often directly related to comfort level with corruption. Familiarity breeds acceptance, and the shorter a politician serves, the less opportunity for nefarious dalliances.

A second possible risk is that voters become so blinded by the need to remove non-reformers that unsuitable opposition will be supported. "Unsuitable" refers to unethical, morally unfit or incompetent candidates (in other words, a continuation of the current crop of politicians). American voters are capable of determining if a candidate is an unreasonable option.

Furthermore, one State Representative or State Senator alone does not have the power to bring our nation to its knees. The risks of inaction are greater than the risks of any wayward candidate winning a seat.

Skeptics, Cynics and Non-Believers

America began as a far-flung colony of peasants and farmers. The odds of defeating the mightiest military in the world to gain our independence were meager. The odds of surviving the brutal bloodletting of our civil war were bleak. Many believe the odds of expelling the Democratic and Republican parties from every corner of our politics are nil. But the underdog moniker is a gift to Americans. It is a badge of honor. It signifies that the piss and vinegar in our veins has yet to be diluted. We revel in being on the business end of a lopsided fight, which is where we find ourselves today.

The task ahead is daunting, but hardly impossible. Simple messaging and a noble cause is all Americans need in order to move worlds. Those who doubt the potential of the proposals herein continue an illustrious line of historical doubters — those whose only contribution to the pantheon of social progress is that of accidental motivator. They provide an invaluable contribution to this grand cause.

Conclusion

We are waiting for a better candidate, for a better system, for a better future. But waiting is not a strategy. It is an excuse for inaction. To wait is to decay, to atrophy, to rot. Either we liberate our government from the tyrants or we continue to whither on the vine. We would hardly be the first nation to suffer a fate of death by noncommittal indignation.

America will never be a land without political parties. This should not be our goal. A free and fair vote is the pinnacle of political expression and should be protected at all costs. This is why we must make a monumental change in our election laws. For too long, we have protected the rights of only two political parties, to the exclusion and detriment of all others. It is *because* the Democrats and Republicans are so powerful that the rights of all other political persuasions are trampled.

Current membership in either party should carry with it a grave stigma — one so powerful that its external pressure demands internal reflection. This is the first key to toppling the tyrants. We must highlight how these two have infected our politics. The average American must recognize that a collective fear of change has led to Republican and Democratic absolute power. Next to our votes, our voices are the most powerful weapons we have in this battle.

The next step is voter empowerment. To recognize that we as voters have the power to remove our oppressors is a liberating concept. We can and must demand change from our leaders, and remove them from office if they do not oblige. They only hold power because we allow them to do so. Such an approach can and will work, if we are disciplined voters. Often times simple name recognition is the determining factor in a toss-up election. Position on electoral reform is a far less trivial single issue for determining the victor of any race.

Liberating America from our two political despots will require courage — not the type of valor that brings revolutionaries to a public square, but strength of will more profound. We must cultivate the stoic resolve of an abused spouse on their way out the door. Fleeing the gravitational pull of an abusive partner is terrifying, but beyond the debilitating fear of the unknown lays true and lasting freedom.

The End

Epilogue

Two Tyrants

An Open Letter to Partisan Voters

Voting Republican today does not make you a modern-day Paul Revere. It is not a vote for liberty but one for elitism and a corrupt bureaucracy. Support for the Republican Party in our current system is a purposeful rejection of our most sacred founding principles. Your vote implies that you would entrust your destiny to willfully ignorant rulers in exchange for the waning bliss of political victory. Such motivations do not build nations, but destroy them.

Voting Democratic in today's environment does not make you a social justice crusader. It does not prove that you care for the underprivileged or the oppressed. It is a conscious vote for the establishment. It simply affirms that you've decided to sit in the third class quarters of the Titanic as she sinks. Dying with the wretched in the bowels is no more righteous than perishing with the nobles in first class. The act may clear your conscience, but it saves no one.

The uncomfortable truth is that neither party has a monopoly on corruption. The Republicans and Democrats are both sustained by the fear they manufacture against each other. That translates into votes for both sides. Most of us are resigned to cast a vote against one of the parties rather than for one of them. The tyrants are perfectly content with maintaining this structure, as it has been the key to their staying power. You must end your participation in this dysfunctional system, for the good of us all.

Every American has the right to life, liberty and the pursuit of happiness. Unfortunately, those in our employ are diminishing the quality of our lives, the breadth of our liberty and our potential for happiness. Our government's public policies have been ruinous, but our election system allows those at fault for these policies to remain.

Your vote can make a difference in the lives of your countrymen, but only if you will cast it for reform of our election process. The Democrats and Republicans care not for your interests. They care only for their power and influence, and they will say anything to maintain it. You can wrest back your political power in the voting booth. Doing so will restore the strength of our democracy.

Two Tyrants

An Open Letter to State Legislators

Thank you for your service to your state. Political parties can be powerful tools for citizen activism. Unfortunately, the Republican and Democratic parties have become a powerful means for unscrupulous people to corrupt our democracy.

For much of our history, social injustices have been vanquished by populist activism. Slavery, denial of female suffrage and corporate trusts all ended because social movements inspired legislation. You have an opportunity to make history as well.

The good people of your state deserve free and fair elections. In its current form, the system only allows two parties fair access to voters. This is neither free nor fair. Please support the following election reforms in your state, which can change the face of our national elections.

1.   Ballot access for all state and federal elections to be reduced to the following parameters: The first four candidates to procure valid petition signatures from five percent of the electorate may appear on the ballot.

2.   Publicly funded party primaries to be replaced by publicly funded four-candidate weighted primaries.

3.   General elections to consist of runoff between two top candidates from open primary.

4.   All state and federal elections including

presidential elections to be strictly non-partisan.

You likely sought elective office due to a commitment to your own ideas. Unfortunately, as an elected Democrat or Republican you have the disadvantage of party loyalty. Your new ideas are likely often rejected and your creativity stifled. We seek to remove the yoke of partisan dogma from your neck and unleash your creative potential.

The framers of our Constitution had the foresight to give you in the state legislatures control over your state's congressional and presidential election process. Our political system is not broken. It's only been commandeered. Please help us regain control through the powers bestowed upon you by the founding fathers. If you do so, you will enjoy great popular support. If you choose not to support electoral reform, you're next opponent will be very grateful.

Two Tyrants

A Note on the Electoral College

Many wish to abolish the Electoral College, and replace it with a strict popular vote. This would be preferable to the Electoral College, as popular presidential voting is a more direct means of selection. The Electoral College forces candidates to strategize and placate to some states over others and encourages that politics trumps leadership.

The only way to abolish the Electoral College is via a Constitutional amendment. In the current environment, an abolition amendment is highly unlikely. The Electoral College is an integral part of the current overlying system on which both tyrants rely. Furthermore, because it is a matter that can only be brought about by congressional passage and presidential signature, it falls outside the confines of the current state solution proposal herein. Nevertheless, passage of the proposed electoral changes outlined here would likely offer a solid first step toward the abolition of the Electoral College.

A.G. Roderick

A Note on Campaign Finance Reform

The current federal campaign finance laws not only favor the two large parties, but also make them virtually unbeatable in the money race. That is the definition of political corruption; a very small minority of people that control all of the money within politics.

Campaign finance is an extremely complex issue, with far-reaching political implications. As with the Electoral College, further campaign finance reform is a federal undertaking and one that is not without monumental challenges. It is a battle wrought with questions of free speech. Although sweeping reforms in campaign financing would be advantageous, it is the right battle at the wrong time. The day will come when the Electoral College and campaign finance reform can be tackled. But we must take the all-important first step of reclaiming our government from the parties before we can move on either of these fronts.

Public-only financing of our elections would be preferable to the current system, but highly unlikely. In a public financed election, those with more money do not necessarily have more influence. It is a means of leveling the playing field.

Two Tyrants

A Note on Proportional Representation

Proportional representation refers to the system of government whereby citizens cast their votes for a party rather than an individual. Some who support election reform support a shift to a proportional representation system. This shift would require a sea change in the manner by which we conduct all of our elections. The changes proposed in chapter three are intended as achievable goals. Not even considering the merits of proportional representation, it is not conceivable that popular support for such a drastic systemic change is on the horizon.

References

[i] *Programme for International Student Assessment (PISA) Results From PISA 2012,* United States (Paris: OECD, 2013).

[ii] Robert Reich, "The Practical Choice: Not American Capitalism or "Welfare State Socialism" But an Economy That's Working for A Few or Many," The Blog, Huffington Post, May 21, 2014, http://www.huffingtonpost.com/robert-reich/american-capitalism-european-socialism_b_5364299.html.

[iii] Alexis de Tocqueville, *Democracy in America* (New York: Penguin, 2003)

[iv] Stephen Dinan, "U.S. debt jumps a record $328 billion - Tops $17 trillion for first time, The Washington Times, October 18, 2013, http://www.washingtontimes.com/news/2013/oct/18/us-debt-jumps-400-billion-tops-17-trillion-first-t/.

[v] "List of American Federal Politicians Convicted of Crimes," Wikipedia, accessed May 14, 2014, http://en.m.wikipedia.org/wiki/List_of_American_federal_politicians_convicted_of_crimes.

[vi] "US Debt Tops 13 Trillion Dollars for First Time," The Economic Times, June 3, 2010, http://articles.economictimes.indiatimes.com/2010-06-03/news/27617617_1_trillion-dollars-debt-government-spending.

[vii] "Reelection Rates Over the Years," OpenSecrets.org, Center for Responsive Politics, accessed February 1, 2014, https://www.opensecrets.org/bigpicture/reelect.php.

[viii] Matt Berman, "Most Members of Congress are Millionaires for the First Time Ever," National Journal, January 9, 2014, http://www.nationaljournal.com/congress/most-members-of-congress-are-millionaires-20140109.

[ix] Arianna Huffington, "Debating the Two-Party System," huffingtonpost.com, February 18, 2011, http://www.huffingtonpost.com/arianna-huffington/debating-the-twoparty-sys_b_824973.html.

[x] Stanley A. Weiss, "Finally the Days of One-Party Rule are Finished in Mexico," The New York Times, September 17, 1997.

[xi] Catalina Camia, "Poll: Political independents Hit Record-High 42%," USA Today, January 8, 2014, http://www.usatoday.com/story/onpolitics/2014/01/08/voters-independent-party-affiliation-gallup/4368925/.

[xii] "Party Affiliation," gallup.com, The Gallup Organization, accessed September 22, 2014, http://www.gallup.com/poll/15370/party-affiliation.aspx.

[xiii] Peyton M. Craighill and Scott Clement, "A Majority of People Don't Like Their Own Member of Congress. For the First Time Ever." The Washington Post, August 5, 2014, http://www.washingtonpost.com/blogs/the-fix/wp/2014/08/05/a-majority-of-people-dont-like-their-own-congressman-for-the-first-time-ever/.

[xiv] Alan Richard, "The Nebraska Way: Non-Partisan Politics Under One Roof," Education Week, May 5, 2004, http://www.edweek.org/ew/articles/2004/05/05/34politics.h23.html.

[xv] "Blanket Primary Axed," CBSNews.com, June 26, 2000, http://www.cbsnews.com/news/blanket-primary-axed/.

[xvi] "Washington's Farewell Address 1796," The Avalon Project, Documents in Law, History and Diplomacy, Yale University, accessed January 8, 2014, http://avalon.law.yale.edu/18th_century/washing.asp.

[xvii] Jeffrey D. Sachs, The Price of Civilization, New York: Random House, 2011.

[xviii] Commission on Presidential Debates Website, "Our Mission," accessed March 13, 2014, http://www.debates.org/index.php?page=about-cpd.

[xix] Commission on Presidential Debates Website, "Commission Leadership," accessed March 13, 2014, http://www.debates.org/index.php?page=commission-leadership.

[xx] Ralph Nader, "Citizen's Debate Commission," The Nader Page, January 17, 2004, accessed June 2, 2014, https://blog.nader.org/2004/01/17/citizens-debate-commission/.

[xxi] Patrick Buchanan, Pat Buchanan on Principle and Values, On the Issues Website, http://www.ontheissues.org/celeb/Pat_Buchanan_Principles_&_Values.htm.

[xxii] Merriam-Webster Online Dictionary, "Propaganda Entry", accessed April 5, 2014, http://www.merriam-webster.com/dictionary/propaganda.

[xxiii] Joseph Burgo, "The Emotional Psychology of A Two-Party System," The Atlantic, March 13, 2013, http://www.theatlantic.com/health/archive/2013/03/the-emotional-psychology-of-a-two-party-system/273906/.

[xxiv] Walter Lippman, Public Opinion, New York: Harcourt, Brace and Co., 1922

[xxv] African Americans and the 15th Amendment, Constitutional Rights Foundation Website, accessed August 22, 2014, http://www.crf-usa.org/black-history-month/african-americans-and-the-15th-amendment.

[xxvi] Eleanor Barkhorn, "'Vote No on Women's Suffrage': Bizarre Reasons For Not Letting Women Vote", The Atlantic, November 6, 2012, http://www.theatlantic.com/sexes/archive/2012/11/vote-no-on-womens-suffrage-bizarre-reasons-for-not-letting-women-vote/264639/.

[xxvii] U.S. Const. art. 4. sec. 1.

52445889R00068

Made in the USA
Lexington, KY
29 May 2016